SCARY PLACES

Creepy Stations

by Dinah Williams

Consultant: Troy Taylor
President of the American Ghost Society

BEARPORT
PUBLISHING

New York, New York

Credits

Cover and Title Page, © Sergey Mironov/Shutterstock, Andrea Michele Piacquadio/Shutterstock, and Yury Asotov/Shutterstock; 4–5, © Kim Jones; 6TL, © Alexander Gardner/Associated Press; 6B, © Bettmann/Corbis / AP Images; 7TR, © Western New York Heritage Press; 7BR, © Charles Brutlag/Shutterstock; 8, © ASSOCIATED PRESS; 9BL, © Daily Mail/Rex / Alamy; 9BR, © FlickrVision; 10, © Troy Taylor; 11L, © Troy Taylor; 11R, © Rolf Hicker Photography / Alamy; 12, © Rolf Hicker Photography / Alamy; 13TR, © Tim_Booth / Shutterstock.com; 13B, © DESHAKALYAN/AFP/Getty Images; 14, © Jim Good; 15, © Bettmann/Corbis / AP Images; 16, © Azad Der-Sarkissian; 17BR, © Viennaslide / Alamy; 17BL, © Michael Kloth/Corbis; 18, 19TL, © Courtesy of The State Archives of North Carolina; 19BL, © Dennis Hallinan / Alamy; 20, © ru:Участник:ComIntern; 21TR, © Shepard Sherbell/CORBIS SABA; 21B, © Tkachev Andrei/ITAR-TASS/Corbis; 22, © Jose Caceres Photography; 23, © Andy Chesney & Debi Baker Chesney; 24, © Sean Pavone / Alamy; 25, © Hospitality Holdings, Inc.; 26, © Alistair Laming / Alamy; 27T, © Hulton Archive/Getty; 27B, © Alistair Laming/LOOP IMAGES/Loop Images/Corbis; 31, © iStockphoto/Thinkstock.

Publisher: Kenn Goin
Editorial Director: Adam Siegel
Creative Director: Spencer Brinker
Design: Dawn Beard Creative
Photo Researcher: Picture Perfect Professionals, LLC

Library of Congress Cataloging-in-Publication Data

Williams, Dinah.
  Creepy stations / by Dinah Williams.
    pages cm. – (Scary places)
  Includes bibliographical references (pages   ) and index.
  ISBN 978-1-61772-749-8 (library binding) — ISBN 1-61772-749-0 (library binding)
  1. Haunted places—Juvenile literature. 2. Ghosts—Juvenile literature. 3. Railroad stations—Miscellanea—Juvenile literature. 4. Railroad terminals—Miscellanea—Juvenile literature. I. Title.
  BF1461.W535 2013
  133.1'22—dc23
                                        2012040284

For more information, write to Bearport Publishing Company, Inc., 45 West 21st Street, Suite 3B, New York, New York 10010. Printed in the United States of America.

10 9 8 7 6 5 4 3 2 1

Contents

Creepy Stations

Most people stop at a station for a brief time when they travel by train or subway. As passengers come and go, the stations are filled with happy greetings, sad good-byes, and the excitement of going on a journey to someplace new. Unfortunately, stations are also often the scenes of disasters or the settings for murders.

Perhaps because so many people and strong emotions come together in these places, many stations are reportedly haunted. Among the 11 creepy stations in this book, you will discover a haunted underground station in London that was used as an **air raid** shelter during **World War II** (1939–1945), a **phantom** train that keeps **plummeting** off a bridge, and a stop along the Pony Express where the sound of horses' thundering hooves can still be heard.

Lincoln's Ghost Train

Exchange Street Station, Buffalo, New York

On April 14, 1865, President Abraham Lincoln was shot in the head while watching a play at Ford's Theatre in Washington, D.C. One week later, a **funeral train** carrying his body left Washington for Springfield, Illinois—the town where Lincoln had lived and would be buried. Although Lincoln's body reached its final destination more than 100 years ago, some say they can still spot his train making stops along its nearly 1,700-mile (2,736 km) route.

About 12 million people—or one-third of the people in the United States—came out to see Lincoln's funeral train during its journey in 1865.

President Abraham Lincoln (1809–1865)

6

The clock struck 7:00 A.M. on April 27, 1865, as Lincoln's funeral train pulled slowly into Exchange Street Station in Buffalo, New York. The black-draped train was six days into its journey. In the last car was the body of the **assassinated** president.

Exchange Street Station

Many **mourners** lined the tracks to catch a glimpse of their fallen leader. Others crowded into the Buffalo station. From there, they followed the coffin to a building called St. James Hall. An estimated 100,000 people viewed Lincoln's body in its open **casket** that day. By 10:00 P.M., the coffin was back on the train, heading to its next stop in Cleveland, Ohio.

That sad day was not the last time the residents of Buffalo saw Lincoln's funeral train, however. Every April, people claim to see the train traveling silently in the night. Its cars are cloaked in black. Guarding the flag-covered coffin are skeletons in blue uniforms. The phantom train is also seen in many other places along the route, but it has never been seen reaching Springfield. Lincoln's ghost, however, has been spotted in Springfield's Oak Ridge Cemetery. Some people have even heard sobbing coming from Lincoln's **tomb**.

People say that clocks stopped whenever Lincoln's funeral train passed through a station in April 1865. Today, it is said that clocks also stop when the ghost train passes through.

Lincoln's tomb,
Oak Ridge Cemetery

Crushed to Death

Bethnal Green Tube Station, London, England

During World War II (1939–1945), Germany was at war with England. As part of their effort to conquer the country, German planes repeatedly dropped bombs on London. During these attacks—known as air raids—**sirens** would go off to warn people to seek safety. Among the places they could go were the underground stations of London's subway system, called the Tube. Who knew that the nineteen steps leading down from the entrance to the Bethnal Green Tube station would be deadlier than enemy bombs?

Steps leading to the Bethnal Green Tube station

On March 3, 1943, an air raid warning sounded at 8:17 P.M. in a part of London known as the East End. Thousands of people ran to the Bethnal Green Tube station so that they could take shelter 80 feet (24 m) below the ground. A single lightbulb lit the staircase at the entrance. People made their way carefully down the steps, which were slippery because it had rained not long before.

Suddenly, a loud noise that sounded like a bomb exploding frightened people on the slippery stairs. One person fell, followed shortly by another. Before either one could get up, other people started helplessly tripping over them. Soon people were **suffocating** in a crush of bodies. Of the 173 victims who died, more than 60 were children.

In the years since, people in the Bethnal Green Tube station have heard the ghostly sounds of the tragedy. In 1981, a station supervisor who was working late heard screams, children sobbing, and the sounds of people panicking. After ten minutes, he fled the station in horror.

People taking shelter in the Bethnal Green Tube station

More than 150,000 people used the stations of the London Tube as air raid shelters during World War II.

Inside the station today

An Unsolved Murder

Wabash Station, Decatur, Illinois

In the early 1900s, Wabash Station was an important stop on the rail line between Detroit, Michigan, and St. Louis, Missouri. While it used to be a busy place, the station is now closed. Only freight trains occasionally pass through town. So who still walks along the tracks at night, looking for criminals? Some say it is the ghost of Omer Davenport.

Wabash Station in the early 1900s

One morning in October 1935, Omer Davenport was working as a railroad **patrolman** outside Wabash Station. After seeing two men jump from a train, he rushed over to investigate. As he chased the men, they both pulled out guns and shot him. Omer was hit in the leg and neck. Although he was taken to Wabash Employees Hospital, Omer died from his wounds soon after he arrived.

Policemen all over the city and county worked hard to try to find the two gunmen. However, Davenport hadn't been able to give a good description of his killers. Even though a reward was offered, the murderers were never found. Many believe this is why Davenport's **spirit** has not been able to rest in peace. Since his death, a mysterious light has been seen bobbing alongside the railroad tracks at night. Some say it is the flashlight of Omer Davenport, still looking for clues that will lead to the men who killed him.

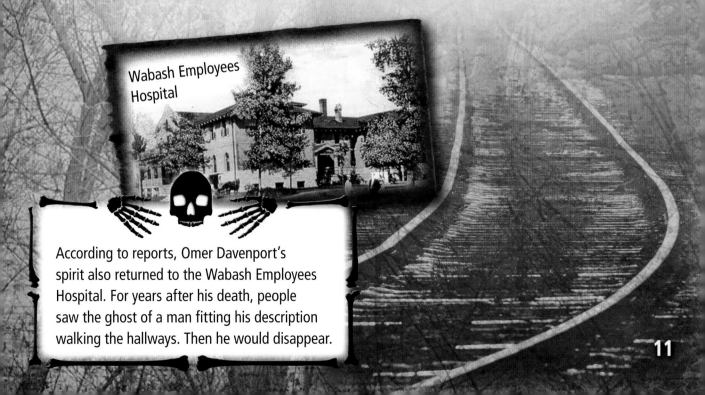

Wabash Employees Hospital

According to reports, Omer Davenport's spirit also returned to the Wabash Employees Hospital. For years after his death, people saw the ghost of a man fitting his description walking the hallways. Then he would disappear.

The Woman in White

Begunkodor Station, Begunkodor, India

For more than forty years, trains passed right through Begunkodor, an out-of-the-way spot in eastern India. Even though people in the area were hoping for a ride, the trains never stopped at the town's brick station. What happened to end train service to the town? Many people believe the station had to be closed because it was haunted.

Begunkodor Station

In 1967, stories began to be told about people who had seen a ghostly woman wearing a white **sari** at Begunkodor Station. Some said she had been killed by a passing train. According to them, a railway worker died after seeing the mysterious figure of the woman in white. As a result of the stories, the other workers lived in fear of seeing her. They were so frightened that they refused to work at the station, which was **abandoned** later that year.

More than four decades passed without any trains stopping at the station. During that time, however, local people pleaded with authorities to have service returned to Begunkodor. In 2009, the station was finally reopened. Still, some people remained concerned. A year later, only one ticket-taker, Dalu Mahato, was working there. Admitting to being spooked by the station, he said, "I make sure that I have friends nearby and make it a point to leave by 6:00 P.M. every day." No one, it seems, wants to be alone with the woman in white.

Not everyone believes that the woman in white exists. Some think that the story was made up by railway workers who didn't want to work in a station that was so far away from other towns and people.

A train speeding past Begunkodor Station

Thundering Hooves

Hollenberg Pony Express Station, Hanover, Kansas

Before railroad tracks crossed America, getting mail to California was difficult. The people who created the Pony Express came up with a solution, however. They hired fast riders to carry mail between more than 180 stations along a 2,000-mile (3,219 km) route that stretched from Missouri—where the existing railroad ended—to California. Although the Pony Express stopped making deliveries more than 150 years ago, some say that one station is still being visited by phantom riders.

Hollenberg Pony Express Station

In 1860, the Pony Express was just getting started. Ads were placed, calling for "young, skinny, wiry fellows . . . willing to risk death daily." The riders needed to be lightweight so the horses could run faster. They also had to be willing to risk their lives because they traveled through rough country, terrible weather, animal attacks, and land that was defended by **Native Americans**. As they neared a station during their danger-filled journeys, riders would shout for a new horse to continue the trip.

A year and a half later, in 1861, the **telegraph** was invented. Since it could deliver messages almost instantly, the Pony Express was discontinued, and most of the stations were abandoned. However, one of the biggest, Hollenberg Station, remained— and according to some, a few ghosts stuck around as well.

Today, Hollenberg Station is a museum. Some visitors and staff members there claim to have heard hooves thundering in the night. They have also heard men yelling for fresh horses. One person reported seeing the spirit of a young man lying on the floor with an arrow in his back. Could he have been the only rider said to have been killed by Native Americans?

A Pony Express rider

In 18 months, Pony Express riders carried 35,000 pieces of mail a total of 650,000 miles (1,046,074 km). Mail from Missouri to California, which normally took nearly a month, arrived in ten days. Only one sack of mail was lost the entire time the Pony Express was in business.

Heart and Soul

Châtelet–Les Halles, Paris, France

For hundreds of years, Paris's Les Halles district was the heart and soul of the city. There, the city's largest outdoor market and its biggest **cemetery** existed side by side. When the area became too crowded, first the cemetery, and then the market, was moved. However, a subway station built on the once jam-packed spot is thought to be overflowing still—with ghosts!

Châtelet–Les Halles
subway station

Les Halles was an open-air market dating back to 1183. Made up of hundreds of food stands, it became known as "the belly of Paris." Each night, thousands of pounds of meat were brought in and butchered. The animals' blood was drained out to the banks of the nearby Seine River.

Next to the market was the Saints Innocents Cemetery. By the 1700s, it had become packed with bodies. Yet people kept burying more. A long rain in 1780 caused a wall next to the cemetery to burst. Bodies spilled out of the cemetery, and the smell was sickening. The king of France ordered burials to be stopped. All of the bodies were moved into mass graves in old **mines** beneath the city.

During the 1970s, the market was moved to a suburb of Paris. The empty space left behind became the Châtelet–Les Halles stop on the Paris subway. Every weekday, approximately 750,000 people go through the station. Some speak of the smell of decay and rot that still lingers from the long-ago cemetery. Others speak of the sounds of ghostly laughter and mysterious whistling in empty train cars.

Inside Châtelet–Les Halles

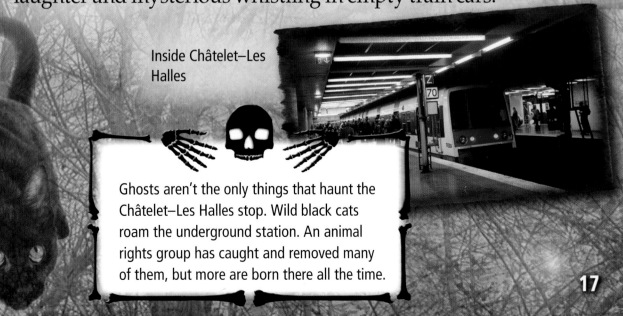

Ghosts aren't the only things that haunt the Châtelet–Les Halles stop. Wild black cats roam the underground station. An animal rights group has caught and removed many of them, but more are born there all the time.

The Wreck of Engine No. 9

Bostian Bridge, Statesville, North Carolina

Engine No. 9 was behind schedule when it left the Statesville station around 2:00 A.M. Picking up speed, it crossed onto Bostian Bridge. The train never made it to the other side, however. The deadly accident that occurred was so terrible it still affects people today.

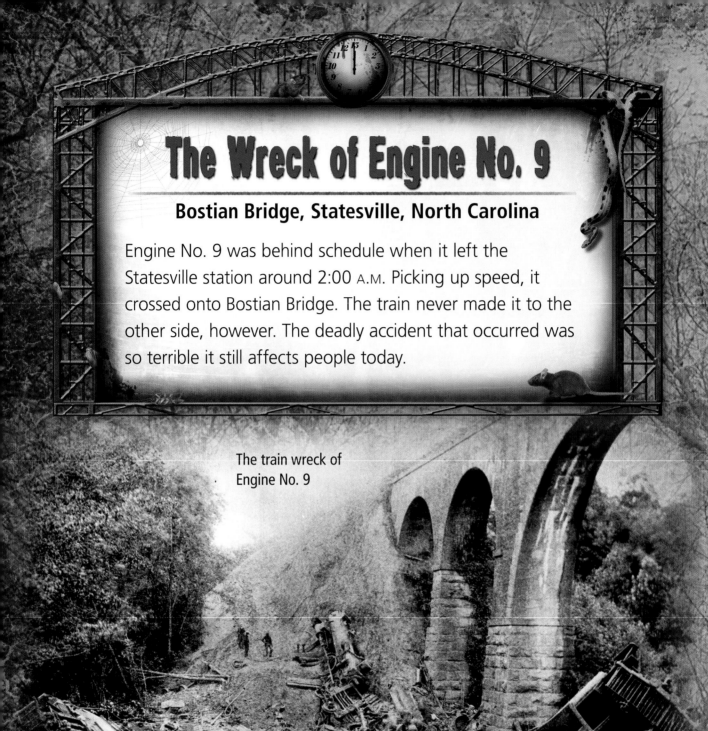

The train wreck of Engine No. 9

Two miles (3.2 km) west of the Statesville station is the site of one of North Carolina's deadliest train wrecks. On August 27, 1891, Engine No. 9 jumped the tracks in the middle of the bridge. The six railcars plunged about 65 feet (20 m) into a creek. Twenty-two people were killed and many others were seriously injured.

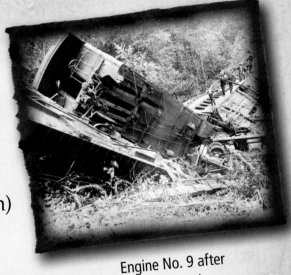

Engine No. 9 after it crashed

Fifty years later, in 1941, a married couple named Larry and Pat Hayes were traveling in the area at night. Their car got a flat tire near the bridge. Larry went to find help. As Pat sat in the car, she noticed a train's light start to cross the bridge. Suddenly, she heard the sounds of screaming and twisted metal. She ran to the scene of the wreck, but the light soon disappeared.

After Pat's husband returned and changed the tire, the couple drove to the Statesville train station to try to figure out what Pat had seen. That's when they learned something shocking from the **stationmaster**—that night was the fiftieth anniversary of the wreck of Engine No. 9. Every year since, the train has been seen plummeting off the bridge on that day.

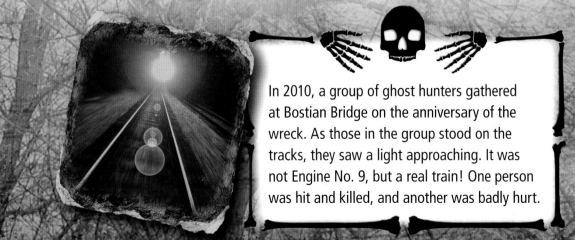

In 2010, a group of ghost hunters gathered at Bostian Bridge on the anniversary of the wreck. As those in the group stood on the tracks, they saw a light approaching. It was not Engine No. 9, but a real train! One person was hit and killed, and another was badly hurt.

Railway of Bones

Salekhard–Igarka Railway, Salekhard, Siberia

Joseph Stalin (1879–1953), **dictator** of the **Soviet Union** from the late 1920s to the early 1950s, ruled with an iron fist. While he was in power, millions of people were unjustly punished by being sent to brutal **labor camps**. A large number of these people ended up in a town called Salekhard, where they were forced to build a railroad line. Unfortunately, many of them never returned home alive.

The Salekhard–Igarka Railway

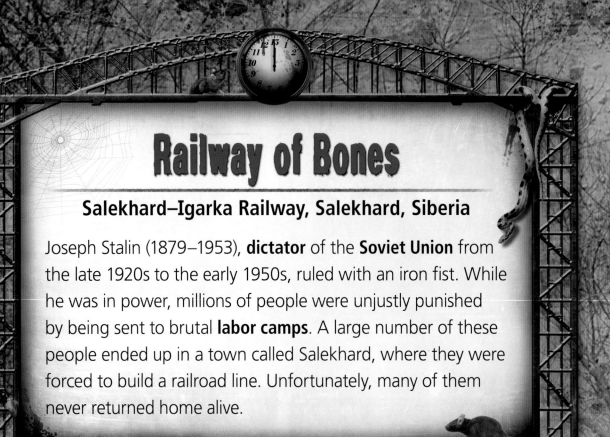

Salekhard, Siberia

Salekhard is located in one of the coldest areas on Earth—the **Arctic**. Between 1949 and 1953, an estimated 300,000 prisoners were sent there. They were forced to build an 806-mile (1,297 km) railway with 28 stations that stretched across Siberia, a huge region in northern Russia.

This was an impossible task. In winter, temperatures dropped down to –76°F (–60°C). Blizzards blew down buildings. Laborers didn't have enough materials, food, or machinery. Most of the work had to be done painfully by hand.

By 1953, with little money and few workers to keep the project going, construction stopped. Only 434 miles (698 km) of railway had been completed, although billions of dollars had been spent. Much of the railway was abandoned. Poorly built tracks were quickly destroyed by frost. Bridges decayed or burned down. At least 11 trains and 60,000 tons (54,431 metric tons) of metal were left to rust. Worst of all, an estimated 100,000 people died building what some called the Railway of Bones and others called the Railroad of Death. Who knows how many sad souls now haunt this cold and empty place?

Lyuba

A different kind of bones can also be found in Salekhard. In 2007, the **mummy** of a 42,000-year-old baby **woolly mammoth**, nicknamed Lyuba, was discovered by a reindeer herder.

A Push to Safety

Corner of Shane and Villamain Roads, San Antonio, Texas

About ten miles (16 km) south of the San Antonio train station is a small railroad crossing. People say that more than sixty years ago it was the site of a deadly train wreck. There hasn't been an accident there since, though. Are spirits from beyond the grave keeping people safe at this crossing?

The railroad tracks that are said to be haunted

According to **legend**, one morning in the 1940s, a school bus that was just outside of San Antonio **stalled** while crossing a section of railroad track. A train moving quickly toward the spot couldn't stop in time and plowed into the bus. Ten children were said to have lost their lives in the horrible crash.

Since then, people say that the ghosts of the dead children haunt the railroad crossing. They are there waiting to protect anyone who gets stuck in the spot where they lost their young lives. Visitors who park a car on the tracks to test out the story witness something strange. They claim that the car travels slowly over the tracks to safety—as though an unseen force is pushing it. If the visitors who are trying the experiment cover the rear bumper with flour or baby powder, small handprints are left behind. Some people also say that they have heard children's voices and laughter, though the crossing is always empty.

A group of teenagers took photos at the crossing. One of the pictures shows the ghostly image of what appears to be a little girl carrying a teddy bear.

The haunted railroad crossing

Not John Campbell

Grand Central Station, New York, New York

Grand Central Station was built in 1913 and is one of the biggest train stations in the world. More than 21 million people pass through this historic building each year. Some people travel there daily for work. Others come to admire the beautiful hand-painted ceilings or eat at one of the restaurants inside the station. One man's spirit, however, arrived at Grand Central years ago—and, some suspect, has never left.

Grand Central Station

In the 1920s, John W. Campbell helped run New York's railroads. He was very, very rich and could afford to rent one of the few offices inside Grand Central Station. Campbell spent a fortune making the enormous room **luxurious**. The office had a chandelier, an organ, and a rare carpet worth hundreds of thousands of dollars.

In 1999, years after Campbell died, the space became a bar. It was named The Campbell Apartment in his honor. Today, owner Mark Grossich and his employees believe that their workplace is home to one or more restless spirits. They have felt gusts of cold air and mysterious taps on their backs. Others have heard the sound of an organ playing.

The Campbell Apartment

Grossich contacted **psychic** Jasmine Hirst to see if she could find out if John Campbell's ghost was haunting the place. In the bar, Hirst saw the spirit of a man with a black mustache wearing a black suit. Grossich then hired **paranormal investigators** to learn more. They asked the spirit if he was the ghost of John Campbell. The investigators' machines picked up the ghostly voice of an irritated man, who said, "No." To this day, the mysterious spirit has never identified himself.

The term "ghost station" doesn't always mean a haunted area. It also refers to stations no longer in use. One of the most beautiful is City Hall Station in the New York City Subway. In 1945, when newer trains that were too long for the old platforms were added to the subway system, the station was closed.

Breezy Bill Is Back

Covent Garden Tube Station, London, England

William Terriss was a popular actor on the London stage in the late 1800s. He easily played both heroes and villains, which earned him the nickname "Breezy Bill." However, Terriss's final role was as the victim of a terrible murder. It is a part his ghost still plays today—in London's Covent Garden Tube station.

Covent Garden
Tube station

On December 16, 1897, William Terriss was walking toward the Adelphi Theatre, where he was appearing in a play. Richard Arthur Prince—a troubled and jealous fellow actor—suddenly stepped out from a doorway. Prince stabbed Terriss twice in the back with a long knife. When Terriss turned around, Prince stabbed him a third time in the chest—and killed him.

Since that shocking murder, Terriss's ghost has been seen repeatedly at the Covent Garden Tube station. In 1955, Jack Hayden was a ticket collector there. He spotted the spirit of a man wearing evening clothes and gloves and carrying a cane. The well-dressed gentleman was walking along the platform and had "a very, very sad face." Hayden later saw the same man climbing a spiral staircase. When Hayden called out to him, the ghost responded with a sad wail.

Actor William Terriss
(1847–1897)

Some in London have asked themselves why Terriss would haunt the station, since it was built ten years after the actor's death. One possible answer has to do with the fact that the station was built on the site of a bakery where Terriss ate every day. Perhaps his ghost is trying to find the place it once knew so well.

Outside Covent Garden

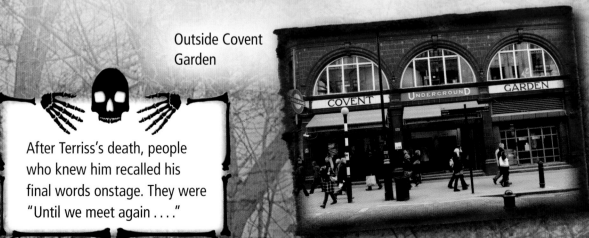

After Terriss's death, people who knew him recalled his final words onstage. They were "Until we meet again . . . ."

Creepy Stations

Wabash Station
Decatur, Illinois

A slain railroad patrolman still hunts for his killers.

Hollenberg Station
Hanover, Kansas

A station on the Pony Express is still visited by long-dead horses and riders.

Crossing at Shane and Villamain Roads
San Antonio, Texas

The spirits of schoolchildren help keep a railroad crossing safe.

Exchange Street Station
Buffalo, New York

Every April, Abraham Lincoln's funeral train retraces the route it took back in 1865.

Grand Central Station
New York, New York

What was once a millionaire's office is now the home of a well-dressed ghost.

Bostian Bridge near Statesville Station
Statesville, North Carolina

A ghost train plummets off a bridge every year.

NORTH AMERICA

SOUTH AMERICA

Pacific Ocean

Atlantic Ocean

Around the World

Salekhard–Igarka Railway
Salekhard, Siberia

Up to 100,000 people died building a "Railway of Bones" leading to nowhere.

Arctic Ocean

Bethnal Green Tube Station
London, England

More than 170 men, women, and children were crushed to death while rushing to safety.

EUROPE

ASIA

Covent Garden Tube Station
London, England

The spirit of a turn-of-the-century actor makes this Tube station his stage.

AFRICA

Châtelet–Les Halles Station
Paris, France

A station on the site of a centuries-old cemetery and market is haunted.

Begunkodor Station
Begunkodor, India

Trains finally return to an abandoned station. Will a ghostly woman return as well?

Indian Ocean

AUSTRALIA

Southern Ocean

ANTARCTICA

Glossary

abandoned (uh-BAN-duhnd) left empty and no longer being used

air raid (AIR RAYD) a bombing from a plane

Arctic (ARK-tik) the northernmost area on Earth

assassinated (uh-SASS-uh-nayt-id) murdered

casket (KASS-kit) a wooden or metal container that a dead person is buried in

cemetery (SEM-uh-*ter*-ee) an area of land where dead bodies are buried

dictator (DIK-tay-tur) a person who has complete control over a country and usually runs it unfairly

funeral train (FYOO-nuh-ruhl TRAYN) a train that carries a coffin to the place where it will be buried

labor camps (LAY-bur KAMPS) places where people who are being punished are forced to work very hard

legend (LEJ-uhnd) a story handed down from long ago that is often based on some facts but cannot be proven true

luxurious (luhk-ZHOOR-ee-uhss) fancy and comfortable

mines (MYENZ) deep holes or tunnels from which rock or other materials are taken

mourners (MORN-urz) people who feel sad because someone has died

mummy (MUH-mee) the preserved body of a dead person or animal

Native Americans (NAY-tiv uh-MER-uh-kinz) the first people to live in America; they are sometimes called American Indians

paranormal investigators (*pa*-ruh-NOR-muhl in-VEST-uh-*gay*-torz) people who study events or collect information about things that cannot be scientifically explained

patrolman (puh-TROHL-muhn) a guard who travels around an area to protect it

phantom (FAN-tuhm) a ghost or spirit

plummeting (PLUHM-it-ing) dropping suddenly

psychic (SYE-kik) a person who communicates with the spirits of dead people

sari (SAR-ee) a large cloth that is draped over a woman's body so that one part forms a skirt and the other part covers the head and shoulders; often worn by women in southern Asia

sirens (SYE-ruhnz) warning devices that make loud, piercing sounds

Soviet Union (SOH-vee-uht YOON-yuhn) a former country that was centered around Russia and had a communist government

spirit (SPIHR-it) a supernatural creature, such as a ghost

stalled (STAWLD) when a vehicle's engine has stopped working

stationmaster (STAY-shuhn-*mas*-tur) the person in charge of running a railroad station

suffocating (SUHF-uh-*kay*-ting) being killed by having one's supply of air stopped

telegraph (TEL-uh-graf) a machine that is able to send messages over long distances using a code of electric signals

tomb (TOOM) a grave, room, or building in which a dead body is buried

woolly mammoth (WUL-ee MAM-uhth) an elephant-like animal that lived thousands of years ago

World War II (WURLD WOR TOO) a worldwide conflict that involved many countries and took place from 1939 to 1945

Bibliography

Austin, Joanne. *Weird Hauntings: True Tales of Ghostly Places.* New York: Sterling (2006).

Holzer, Hans. *Ghosts: True Encounters with the World Beyond.* New York: Black Dog & Leventhal (2005).

Rule, Leslie. *Coast to Coast Ghosts: True Stories of Hauntings Across America.* Kansas City, MO: Andrews McMeel Publishing (2001).

Read More

Hawes, Jason, and Grant Wilson. *Ghost Hunt: Chilling Tales of the Unknown.* New York: Little, Brown and Company (2010).

Osborne, Mary Pope, and Natalie Pope Boyce. *Ghosts.* New York: Random House Children's Books (2009).

Teitelbaum, Michael. *Ghosts and Real-Life Ghost Hunters.* New York: Scholastic (2008).

Learn More Online

To learn more about creepy stations, visit
www.bearportpublishing.com/ScaryPlaces

Index

About the Author

Dinah Williams is an editor and children's book author. Her books include *Shocking Seafood; Slithery, Slimy, Scaly Treats; Monstrous Morgues of the Past; Haunted Houses*; and *Spooky Cemeteries*, which won the 2009 Children's Choice Award. She lives in Cranford, New Jersey.